Dedicated to my grandchildren.

The thing about leaves.

By Jacqueline Robertson-Yeo

Copyright © 2023 Jacqueline Robertson-Yeo
All rights reserved.

Cover design by Jacqueline Robertson-Yeo

Book design by Jacqueline Robertson-Yeo

No part of this book can be reproduced in any form or by written, electronic or mechanical, including photocopying, recording, or by any information retrieval system without written permission of the author.

Published by Swifty's Adventures

Printed by IngramSpark UK

Printed worldwide.

Although every precaution has been taken in the preparation of this book, the publisher and author assume no responsibility for errors or omissions. Neither is any liability assumed for damages resulting from the use of information contained herein.

ISBN 978-1-7393238-2-0

The thing about leaves

Written & Illustrated by
Jacqueline Robertson-Yeo

The thing about leaves... that grow on trees,

They are all shapes, colours, and sizes... you see.

They remove harmful gases... would you believe?

Even giving us the fresh air that we need to breathe.

They change colour to let us know... by the way,

...that the start of a new season is on its way.

Leaves are food for insects, and some animals too.

And can be compost for plants, for seedlings to grow through.

For some small bugs, leaves are their home...

...a playground, place to sit, crawl under and roam.

Bugs dwell beneath leaves to hide away...

and use leaves to find shelter, away from the rain.

Leaves can be musical... listen as they rustle in the wind.

Or watch, as leaves carry seeds to the ground...

as they spiral and spin.

Fallen leaves can make quite a mess on the ground.

Have fun in the park as you kick them around.

Enjoy sticking fallen leaves on paper with glue.

It's fun to help tidy fallen leaves away too.

The End.

Other books written & illustrated by
Jacqueline Robertson-Yeo

www.jrobertson-yeo.co.uk

www.ingramcontent.com/pod-product-compliance
Lightning Source LLC
Chambersburg PA
CBHW040023130526
44590CB00036B/72